the REVELATION *of* REVELATION

The Book of Revelation - A Total Fraud

Ken Vernon and Brooke Folk

ISBN: 978-1-954341-68-5 (Paperback)

Writers' Branding
1800-608-6550
www.writersbranding.com
orders@writersbranding.com

Contents

DEDICATION

To our Creator we dedicate this special work. Though a small work in comparison to your mighty works, we acknowledge that even this inspired work came from you through your Holy Spirit, using these humble vessels, ordinary folks.

There is no little works in your eyes but beginnings. Recordings of your divine purpose through your chosen inspired leaders throughout your timelines have inspired and confounded. Tablets of stone to scrolls to printed Bibles and now the electronic tablets that bring your end time message globally is evidence of information running rampant in the end of the ages.

The myths, the legends, the traditions of men, the portrayers of Bible stories on big screens have mystified and mislead as entertainment for the masses. Now to those who have an ear to hear, this simple work will astound all who have been seeking understanding. Unlocking understanding as you have declared would come to those first fruits who seek your truth in the end times. Not the end of this earth but the beginning, the coming of your Kingdom here on this earth.

The tampering of passages of scripture that you have warned against have mislead nations into doom, gloom, and confusion and are now being exposed by your inspired revelation of the scriptures revealing the truth. Through it all, this small humble work, as a mustard seed will grow with Your inspired might and reveal the Gospel, the good news that you have intended since creation. Amein

Your humble servants.

ABOUT THE AUTHOR/WRITER

Isaiah 28:10 (KJV): *For precept must be upon precept, precept upon precept; line upon line, line upon line; here a little, and there a little.*

The Revelation of Revelation is a story never told before now because it wasn't to be told until now according to scriptures. It didn't happen in a vision, not in a sudden rush of a mighty wind, but instead a gentle but profound inspiration.

Ken Vernon has had this respect for the scripture that says if you continue in my word, you shall know the truth, and he is the one to whom this message has been given. He knows his way around the books of the Bible and the messages within. But a mighty message that has confounded is now being revealed.

Brooke Folk an inspired writer since 2007 has had a twenty-five-year friendship association with Ken based on the study of scriptures that began in the summer of 1987 in Melville, New York, at a union hall where church services in Suffolk County were being held for the then Worldwide Church of God.

Their background was and is uniquely based on and around their need to know. Each seeking answers about the true meaning of the Bible. Ken needs to see it in scripture, and Brooke continuously asks for simplicity in all things.

It is in their seeking, their asking, that more than much has now been given. Ken in his revealing scripture knowledge and Brooke in understanding through this simplified message that many will come to understand through a simplified writing style. There is now a shared feeling that we are living in the end times. Not the end of the earth and civilization with all that doom and gloom of Revelation but the end of a time and a time of renewing.

Many will come seeking, many will remember the scriptures of their childhood; ask and it shall be given. Many will be drawn to this revealing through no crafty sleight of hand or words fabricated by Ken or cleverly formatted within these pages. There is no church being built, no tithes and offerings begged for. There are no denominations, affiliations, just the inspired plain truth of a mighty revelation that will upset many, perhaps, but release the false bondage of false teaching to all who have an ear to hear.

For those who doubt these words or to those who would like to have issue with their lack of credentials or a simplified style of writing in presenting this important work, both Ken and Brooke admit that they don't have a leg to stand on in degrees, and they can't boast about their robes or phylacteries **(Matthew 23:5 KJV),** but Ken does have the inspired word that can't be refuted. Now line upon line, this work is presented unto you, *The Revelation of Revelation*. Keep in mind that the following scriptures are given to you as their only credentials:

Isaiah 66:2 (NKJV): *But on this one will I look: On him who is poor and of a contrite spirit, And who trembles at My word.*

Matthew 11:25 (CJB): *It was at that time that Yeshua said, "I thank you, Father, Lord of heaven and earth, that you concealed these things from the sophisticated and educated and revealed them to ordinary folks.*

Ken Vernon, ***the inspired receiver, author and presenter of The Revelation of Revelation.***

Brooke Folk, writer (an ordinary folk), for the publishing and promoting of *The Revelation of Revelation.*

PREFACE

Many commentaries and books about the Book of Revelation exist today. Why, then, one might ask, do we need to have another?

All those responsible for the previous works fail to see, that the Book of Revelation is a fraudulent document. That is the primary reason no one has been able to explain its many complicated passages, after much toil for centuries.

The obvious question, then, is who are we to make a radical statement of such magnitude?

The answer is rather simple. Using the scriptures as our guide, we will demonstrate how this is done.

This book will guide the reader, in a manner, which cannot be found, in any other work that has been written about the Book of Revelation, nor for that matter, any other book in the Bible.

We will not attempt to explain any of the mysterious passages found written in the book, but!

We will provide you with proof, showing, that the Book of Revelation is a fraudulent document, and also show you, how to go about following the instructions written in the Bible, in order to come to the place of the knowledge of the truth and not by trying to interpret what's written in it.

From the prophet Isaiah we learn, to whom knowledge would be taught, and here are those instructions, from Isaiah 28 and verse 9 (KJV):

> Whom shall he teach knowledge? and whom shall he make to understand doctrine? [The answer begins here] them that are weaned from the milk, and drawn from the breasts.

Verse 10:

> For precept must be upon precept, precept upon precept; line upon line, line upon line; here a little, and there a little.

By following those instructions, we are able to share knowledge with you, line upon line, and at the same time, provide you with all the scriptures that you need so that you can do your own independent fact-checking of the scriptures, line upon line, precept upon precept, as you read, or anytime you so desire.

Here are some more scriptures to emphasize the importance of trusting the scriptures to bring you to the place of the knowledge of the truth.

From the Gospel of John chapter 8 and verse 31 (KJV):

Then said Jesus to those Jews which believed in him, If ye continue in my word, then are ye my disciples indeed;

Verse 32:

And ye shall know the truth, and the truth shall make you free.

From another passage of scripture, we learn and I quote, "I am the way the life and the truth." Those words are from the Messiah himself, found in the Gospel of John.

One more scripture from the prophet Isaiah, chapter 66 and verse 2 (NKJV), latter part:

> But on this one will I look: On him who is poor and of a contrite spirit, And who **trembles at My word.**

It is by virtue of treating the words of the creator with the utmost respect that we boldly proclaim the Book of Revelation to be a total fraud.

By sharing the scriptures above with you, we demonstrated the line upon line, precept upon precept principle.

The scriptures were not meant to be understood by the world, contrary to popular opinion. The Messiah prayed for his people in the Gospel of John the night before he was crucified.

Here are some words from that prayer, from John 17, verse 9 (KJV): *I pray for them: I pray not for the world, but for them which thou hast given me; for they are thine.*

In that prayer, he made it crystal clear that the world was not included. Again contrary to popular belief that the Creator is trying to save the world. Now to the role of the Holy spirit in the church, and I will once again use the scriptures to demonstrate this most important point.

> John 14:15: *If you love me you will keep my commands,*
>
> Verse 16 (CJB): *and I shall ask the Father, and he will give you another comforting counselor like me **the Spirit of truth** to be with you **forever.***
>
> Verse 17 (KJV): *Even the **Spirit of truth** which the world cannot receive.* **[Proof that the world cannot receive the truth.]**
>
> Acts 5 and verse 32 (KJV): *and we are his witnesses of these things; and also is the **Holy Spirit whom God hath given to them that obey him.***
>
> From the scriptures we learn the truth, line upon line, precept upon precept, here a little and there a little.

And there, in brief, we shared with you the reason that mainstream religion cannot learn the truth from the scriptures. Neither did they learn the **TRUTH about the Book of Revelation.**

Here is our final scripture, John 17 and verse 17 (KJV): Sanctify them through thy **TRUTH:** thy word is TRUTH.

ACKNOWLEDGMENT PAGE

We go back to our earthly beginnings with great appreciation to our parents and for every life that has touched ours to this very day. The days that marked our adulthood number well over fifty years in which we began to read scriptures. That calling has been misunderstood for decades but has now become clear through inspired knowledge. To all who have instructed us with their wisdom of scriptures and touched our desire to seek the truth and understanding through scriptures rather than the traditions of men, in hindsight, we see and appreciate the knowing that was necessary.

Even to those who unknowingly or knowingly irked our desire and became arguably in disagreement, we thank you. It was those uncomfortable confrontations that gave us resolve and strength in being steadfast in our quest for the truth. The centuries of Bible translations were necessary in keeping the multitudes of followers of their faith increasing and learning, but at the same time, with feelings of an emptiness and confusion by the vast numbers of translations and the gnawing frustrations regarding which one was the right one. All the confusion evidenced in these very end times is acknowledged, with full understanding that it was allowed and prophesied.

To our closest loved ones and friends who helped in nurturing the many questions you wanted scripture answers for, we thank you. To the thousands and tens of thousands who have been responsible in bringing this Internet to fruition, it may astound you to know that your efforts were inspired as well and is now making possible the distribution of this work at great speed around the globe.

We also acknowledge those who began and maintain our revelation of revelation radio broadcast at TalkShoe.com. Thank you

The Publisher of this one-of-a-kind work had nothing to compare it to, but through diligence, it was prepared for digital reading on many devices including tablets.

To our Creator, we give all the praises for this revealing in the simplicity of the truth that comes from the scriptures themselves.

Ken Vernon and Brooke Folk

CHAPTER 1

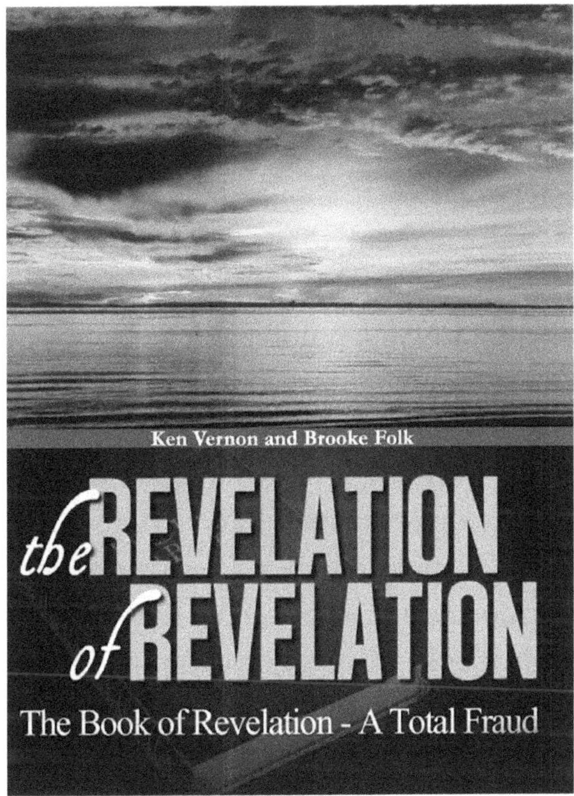

For centuries, people from various walks of life have examined and studied the contents of the Book of Revelation. It has been a mystery and a puzzle to all. Volumes of books have been written about the Book of Revelation, attempting to explain its mysterious passages.

NOTE: 883,000 commentaries have been written on the Book of Revelation according to a recent query using a major search tool.

For all the efforts over hundreds of years, there has never been an answer that is the accepted truth or explanation. Not one. By being drawn to this book, you have been given an open invitation to join us in our unique approach to **The Revelation of Revelation.**

Here is a command from the Messiah to his disciples. *Go you therefore into **All** the world and preach the Good news to every creature.* He gave that command to the eleven: **Mark 16 verses 14–20**. The writers of the Book of Revelation tells us that he gave to the Apostle John seven letters to be given to the seven churches in Asia. The other churches wherever they were at this time were doing a splendid job. No need for any course correction so the events which were shortly to come would not have any effect on them. Also, there was no need to tell them anything about the future. *Major problem!*

We are told in the Gospel of **John 3 verse 16:** *for God so loved the world that he gave his only begotten Son, that whosoever believeth in him shall not perish but have everlasting life.* He loves the world, but according to the writer(s) of the Book of Revelation, He is about to rain down holy hell on all mankind, for five months, unless of course you belong to one of the twelve tribes of the children of Israel, and you are among the 144,000 listed in chapter 7 verses 3 through 8. See also chapter 9 verse 10.

No warning to the world that he is unhappy with mankind, only to the seven churches in Asia. Does that not seem absurd? The writer(s) of the Book of Revelation would have us believe that those sinister events were about to unfold on **all mankind.** First he sends the Apostles, no less than twelve of them, to proclaim **GOOD NEWS,** and then he sends one of the twelve, to reverse his original command but only to the seven churches in Asia.

That is totally insane. The Creator is not a man. *He does not lie.* **Heb. 6:18** (KJV). First, good news, and then followed by bad news? **IMPOSSIBLE!**

In the book of the prophet Jonah, you will find a perfect example showing how the Creator works with mankind. Very briefly here is what we find in the book of the Prophet Jonah. Jonah was sent to the people of Nineveh to warn them of pending disaster if they failed to clean up their act. The people took corrective action and spared themselves a beating from the hands of the Creator. That is how He works. He never whacks anyone without a warning. Read the book; we highly recommend that you do.

That makes sense, even on the human level. We advise children in like manner in the way they should go. Never does the Most High do anything in an arbitrary manner. He always sends a warning first. Sometimes He does it repeatedly as in the case of the children of Israel. He gives the people a chance to clean up their act. Why, because he loves the world, not because he hates it. The writers of the Book of Revelation would have us believe just the opposite.

Here is where the fun begins. Who is responsible for this CONCOCTION that they have the temerity to label Revelation? We will reveal this to you, along with how they unwittingly reveal themselves to the entire world and catch this. It will be revealed to you **who the people are today who have followed them.**

Let's begin by sharing a few very pertinent scriptures. John 17:17 (NKJV): *Sanctify them by Your truth. Your word is truth.* Another rendering found in the CJB, the complete Jewish Bible by David Stern: *Set them apart* for holiness by means of the truth—your word is truth.

Clarity is unmistaken. By virtue of the TRUTH, the word of truth is found only in the scriptures, and from them, we are able to distinguish between that which is true and that which is not. We cannot rely on any man to bring us to that truth. That includes the author/writer of this book. **No exceptions!**

Let us continue with the scriptures as our guide.

John 14:6 (CJB): *Yeshua said, "I AM the Way — and the Truth and the Life;*

The Messiah labels himself the Truth. Again clarity is unmistaken. Sterns: CJB.

Jeremiah 17:5 (NKJV): *Cursed is the man who trusts in man.*

The Creator pronounces a curse on any man who puts his trust in another human being. If we don't heed those words from our maker, it is not possible to determine truth from lies. We continue to prove this vital point.

John 8:31 (KJV): *Then said Jesus to those Jews who believed on him, If ye* ***continue in my word****, then are ye my disciples indeed; And* ***ye shall know the truth****, and the* ***truth shall make you free.***

Again, the truth comes from the Messiah (the one who called himself the Truth), as we showed you earlier. We demonstrate our obedience by continuing in his word, and by doing so, he rewards us with the knowledge of the **Truth**.

John 14:15–16 (NKJV): "If you love Me, keep My commands. And I will pray the Father, and He will give you another Helper, that He may abide with you forever—

How long? Forever!

CHAPTER 2

THE HOLY SPIRIT REVEALS THE FUTURE

John 14:15 (CJB): *"If you love me, you will keep my commands;* **16** *and I will ask the Father and he will give you another comforting Counselor like me, the Spirit of Truth, to be with you* ***forever.***

John 14:25 (CJB): *"I have told you these things while I am still with you;* **26** *But the Counselor, the* Ruach HaKodesh, *whom the father will send in my name, will teach you everything; that is, he will remind you of* ***everything*** *I have said to you.*

John 16:13 (CJB): *However, when the Spirit of Truth comes, he will guide you into all the truth; for he will not speak on his own initiative but will say only what he hears. He will also announce to you the events of the future.* **Here is the bombshell! Get Ready!** *He will also announce to you the* ***events of the future!***

Note: The scripture above clearly stipulates, the revelation of future events would come to us by the Holy Spirit. Not from any other source. We cannot rely on human agency to bring us the creator's truth. From Jeremiah 17 verse 5, the creator pronounces a curse on any man who puts his trust in another man. Question: Why would he?

You are about to learn the mystery of the Book of Revelation, the book that has plagued and puzzled many wise men and scholars before us for almost two thousand years. Let's begin the Revelation of Revelation

Revelation 1:1 (CJB): *This is the revelation which God gave to Yeshua the Messiah, so that he could show his servants what must happen very soon.*

The KJV translates that passage as follows: *The Revelation of Jesus Christ, which God gave unto him, to shew unto his servants things which must shortly come to pass.*

Here is where we all missed the smoking gun! The writer begins his narrative by telling us that there is now a new system for communicating with the church. He (or they) indicates that God the Father must now do the revealing to God the Son. A new system has been put in place. God and Christ are no longer one. In the Gospel of John, as we showed earlier, the Apostle John wrote: **I and my Father are one. The spirit of truth, as promised, has been replaced.**

In Ephesians, we are told Christ is the Head of the Body/church. It's his Body, but! According to the writer(s) of revelation, he is not aware of what's going on in His own Body.

They would have us believe, the Book of Revelation was written by the Apostle John. John wrote in the Gospel of John that the spirit of truth would guide us into all truth, would show us **Future events**. Who in his or her right mind would accuse the Spirit of Truth of telling lies?

In the following chapters, we will show the readers a host of lies that further demonstrates this fraudulent work. The only revelation in the Book of Revelation is the revelation of Lies! **The lies were fashioned to control and manipulate the people.**

In Proverbs 30:6 (KJV), *we read, Add thou not unto his words, lest he reprove thee, and thou be found* ***liar.***

The book fails the litmus test right at the start. It is nothing but lies! **Note:** God does not reveal anything to God. God is God! Moses wrote in **Deut. 6:4 (KJV)**: *Hear, O Israel: The Lord our God is one Lord.* The Gospel of **John 10:30 (KJV)** reaffirms that and reads: *I and my Father are one.*

Comment: In several passages in the New Testament, we find evidence of the religious authority of the day, seeking an opportunity to stone him to death for declaring the oneness of Father and Son. At his trial, that was the charge they brought against him. They had witnesses to back up their charge.

In **Genesis 1:26,** we read, *And God said, Let us make man in our image, after our likeness*: ***Note:*** *Let us,* **not** let me, clearly showing that Christ is God and the Father is God. This also accords with the scripture we find in the Gospel of John. **Chapter 1 and verse 1:** ***In the beginning was the Word, and the Word was with God, and the Word was God.***

In verse 10, we read, He was in the world, and the world was made by him, and the world knew him not.

Yet the revelation writer(s) would have us believe that he needs to have present and future events, revealed to him by the other God.

CHAPTER 3

MORE LIES!

John was told to write down as much as he saw: **Revelation 1:2 (CJB):** *and send those letters to the seven churches which are in Asia, by seven messengers, for the time is near.* All the people to whom these letters were sent died more than 1900 years ago.

Their children died, their grandchildren died, their great-grandchildren died, and so on and so on. That should be obvious to anyone who has ever read the Book of Revelation. We know the Messiah never came, and there was no hell and destruction on mankind.

In Revelation 1:7 (KJV), the writer(s) makes a bold proclamation: *Behold, he cometh with clouds.* Reading the Book of Revelation for the first time and seeing those words, one might draw the conclusion that the writer is seeing the Messiah in this vision, coming with the clouds of heaven.

But! For those who are familiar with the Gospels, he or she knows those words can be found in the Gospel of **Matthew 24:30** and in at least two or three other passages, such as **Mark 13:26 and 14:62, and** in the book of Daniel and other Old Testament books.

Matthew 24:30: *Then the sign of the Son of man will appear in the sky, all the tribes of the land will mourn and they will see the Son of man* ***coming on the clouds of*** *heaven with tremendous power and glory.*

Those words were spoken by the Messiah himself to his disciples as they sat upon the Mount of Olives. The scripture clearly says "his disciples." The apostle John was present at the time. He then, heard the messiah speak those words.

In **Matthew 24:3 (KJV)** we read: *And as he sat upon the mount of Olives, the disciples came unto him privately, saying, Tell us, when shall these things be? and what shall be the sign of thy coming and of the end of the world?*

Note: His disciples came to him privately.

Comment: The writer begins his narrative by indicating that the instruction given to him was to write down as much as he saw.

Then he continues to quote a passage of scripture that was recorded by several prophets centuries earlier. You can find them in your old testament. Any study version of the scriptures will prove that to you.

Next he begins to record what he heard, a clear case of not following the instructions he was given, or this is where the lies begin, in clear violation of the instructions. The angel was instructed to pass on the revelation of future events in a vision, not by voice. Chapter 1 clearly shows such was the case. The writer indicates that the Messiah in this vision actually touched him. And spoke to him. If that be the case, the Messiah was speaking to him, what is the purpose of the angel in the vision?

That event took place in 33 AD/CE. Since John was already aware of that fact, why would he, some sixty years later in AD/CE 96, the Year when the historians tell us that the Book of Revelation was written,write those words in a book, pretending that he is seeing them in a vision, from that angel? This is nothing short of ignorance of scriptures.

He was instructed to write down as much as he saw and send those letters to the seven churches in Asia. All this came by revelation according to the writer, from Father to Son, to an Angel, and finally in the form of a vision to the Apostle John.

John was banished to the Isle of Patmos as the writer(s) claims, for preaching the Gospel. But now he is instructed to find seven messengers and send each one to the seven churches. Here we find the spirit of truth is not involved; the job is given to mortals. Contrary to what we read in the Gospel of John.

What a task for an old man in his nineties who is living in a state of banishment without any income? Nevertheless let us continue to show you the madness that is written in the book.

The seven churches in Asia on the continent would have to be reached first by boat from the Isle of Patmos and then, by some other means of transportation or on foot. These letters were of grave importance. This was an urgent matter because the Messiah was coming soon, and they had some spiritual issues that required urgent attention; otherwise their candle sticks would be removed.

Question? Where else in the Bible do we find this kind of nonsense? The Creator of the Universe and everything in it is keeping track of the churches with candlesticks. What Nonsense! But it doesn't stop there.

Note: All the instructions given to the churches were verbal commands; not one came in the form of a vision, once again a clear violation of the instructions we find in chapter 1.

The church in Philadelphia, and this is the clincher, does not have any issues whatsoever. They were doing a splendid job as we read in **Revelation 3:7–13 (CJB),** but the writer(s) would have us believe that the Messiah/Yashua, the WORD, God, who is God, has no knowledge of this whatsoever; the Father had to reveal it to him. Do you see the madness?

The writer(s) would have us believe that it requires a revelation from Father to Son/ God to God, and then to an Angel into a vision and then to the apostle John, which he would write down, from the vision on paper seven times, and then given to seven messengers to deliver them by sea and then overland to the seven churches. Nowhere in the Bible do we find that kind of nonsense when the Creator communicates with His people. He sends his prophets as in the days of the Old Covenant. The scriptures clearly state that the spirit of truth will communicate all truth and knowledge of future events to the church.

Not through human agency.

> In chapter 2, we shared with you exactly how the Creator communicates with his people.

Here, for emphasis, is the scripture once again.

John 16:13 from (Dr. **Stern's C**omplete **J**ewish **B**ible): *However, when the Spirit of Truth comes, he will guide you into all the truth; for he will not speak on his own initiative but will say only what he hears. He will also announce to you the* ***EVENTS*** *of the* ***FUTURE.***

The passage above from Revelation is the trash you and I bought into along with other Bible students, scholars, theologians, and Clergymen alike for the past 1700 years or more.

The time has come for the truth to be told. In **Daniel 12:4** (CJB)**,** the prophet was told to keep the words secret and seal up the book until the time of the end. This shall be a time when many would rush here and there as knowledge increases. This is **where we are! At the time of the end!**

Here are some key scriptures which has never been referenced or quoted by any of the other books or articles written about the Book of Revelation.

Habakkuk 2 and verse 1 **(NIV):**

I will stand at my watch *and station myself on the ramparts; I will look to see what he will say to me, and what answer I am to give to this complaint.*

Verse 2: *Then the lord replied: "Write down the **Revelation,** and make it plain on **TABLETS** so that a herald may run with it.*

Verse 3: *For the **revelation** awaits an appointed time; it speaks of the **end**, and will not prove false, though it linger, wait for it; it will certainly come and will not delay.*

And there we have it, the revelation of revelation awaited an appointed time when it would be presented on TABLETS. Never before this time in the history of the world was this possible. The scriptures, clearly states, it awaited an appointed time it speaks of the **END.**

Note: From the Gospel of John, we are told that the world cannot receive the spirit of truth. See John 14 and verse 17. Small wonder no one saw it before.

More about the Holy Spirit.

The Holy Spirit functions in the church in the same manner as the Sabbath day, in the nation of Israel during the days of the first Covenant, in the land of Israel, the Promised Land.

Exodus 31:12 (NKJV): And the LORD spoke to Moses, saying, **13** "*Speak also to the children of Israel, saying: 'Surely My Sabbaths you shall keep, for it is a **Sign** between Me and you throughout your generations, that you may know that I am the LORD who sanctifies you.'"* **17** *It is a **sign** between Me and the children of Israel forever.* The Sabbath, then, was an identifying sign between the Holy One of Israel and his people.

Now to the church and the Holy One of Israel. On the Day of Pentecost/first-fruits, when that day came in 33 AD/CE, here is what we are told from the book of **Acts 2:1 (KJV):** *When the day of Pentecost/**first-fruits** had fully come, they were all with one accord in one place. And suddenly there came a sound from heaven as of a mighty rushing wind and it filled the whole house where they were sitting.* ***3*** *Then there appeared to them divided tongues, as of fire and one sat upon each of them.* ***4*** *And they were all filled with the Holy Spirit and began to speak with other tongues, as the **spirit** gave them utterance.*

Let's move forward to verse **12**: *so they were all amazed and perplexed, saying to one another, "Whatever could this mean?" but Peter standing up with the eleven* **14** *lifted up his voice and said unto to them. Ye men of Judea and all ye that dwell at Jerusalem, be this known unto you and hearken to my words:* **15** *For these are not drunken as ye suppose* **16** *But this is that which was spoken by the prophet Joel; And it shall come to pass in the last days, saith*

God, I will pour out my Spirit upon all flesh and your sons and your daughters shall prophesy and your young men shall see visions and your old men shall dream dreams.

The purpose for sharing the scriptures above is to highlight the significance of the signs used by the Creator to identify and communicate with his people.

Comment: From the scriptures above, we can see how the writers of the Book of Revelation display a total lack of respect for the words of the Creator and treats them with the utmost contempt.

We would be remiss if we didn't share this scripture found in **Isaiah 66:2 (NKJV):** *"For all those things my hand has made and all those things exist," says the LORD. "But on this one will I look: On him who is poor and of a contrite* **spirit,** *and who trembles at my word.*

Note: He did not say, the priest or the minister or any clergy person.

CHAPTER 4

MORE SCRIPTURE EXAMPLES FROM ACTS

Skeptics need more assurance. Additional extremely important scriptures for additional support are found in Acts.

Acts 15:36 (NKJV): *Then after some days Paul said to Barnabas, "Let us now go back and visit our brethren in every city where we have preached the word of the Lord and see how they are doing."*

Acts 16:1 (NKJV): *Then he came to Derbe and Lystra. And behold, a certain disciple was there, named Timothy,* (first part of that verse.) Verses **2** and **3** shows that Timothy joins Paul and Silas. (See Acts 15:40, NKJV, where Barnabas and Paul had contentions.)

Continuing in **Acts 16:5 (NKJV):** *So the churches were strengthened in the faith and increased in number daily.* **6** *Now when they had gone through Phrygia and the region of Galatia, they were forbidden by the* ***Holy Spirit*** *to preach the word in Asia.* **That is the only way he communicates with the church.** There is more evidence. Verse: **7:** *After they had come to Mysia, they tried to go into Bithynia but the* ***Spirit*** *did not permit them.*

Comment: Here we have two perfect examples of the Holy Spirit working with the Apostle to the Gentiles.

Verse 8: *So passing by Mysia, they came down to Troas.* **9** *And a vision appeared to Paul in the night. A man of Macedonia stood and pleaded with him saying "come over to Macedonia and help us."* **10** *Now after he had seen the vision, immediately we sought to go to Macedonia, concluding that the Lord had called us to preach the gospel to them.* This was in a vision directly to the Apostle for him and his companions. There was no secondhand message by human agency involved here.

In Ephesians, Saul (Paul) had this to say to the congregation. **Ephesians 1:11 (CJB):** *also in union with him we were given an inheritance we who were picked in advance according to the purpose of the one who effects everything in keeping with the decision of his will,* **12** *so that we who earlier, had put our hope in the Messiah would bring him praise commensurate with His glory.*

Now Verse 13: *Furthermore, you who heard the message of the truth, the Good News (Gospel) offering you deliverance and put your trust in the Messiah were sealed by him with the promised Ruach HaKodesh, (Holy Spirit)* **14** *who guarantees our inheritance until we come into possession of it and thus bring him praise commensurate with his glory.* **Yes, we who respond to the gospel** (The Good News) are identified by the Holy **Spirit.**

Remember! Mark 16:15–17: *Go you therefore into all the world and preach the Good News and these* ***signs*** *will accompany those who believe. They shall cast out demons in my name, they shall lay hands upon the sick, and the sick shall be made well,* etc., that, in essence, is what the Apostle Paul explained to the Ephesian congregation.

That sealing goes with us into the grave and beyond, right into the Kingdom. That's when we receive our inheritances. In the book of **Hebrews** in **chapter 11: verse 13 we read,** all these people kept on trusting until they died, without receiving what had been promised. **Hebrews 11:39 (CJB)** (latter part): *Nevertheless, they did not receive what had been promised.* **40** *Because God had planned something better that would involve us, so that only with us would they be brought to the goal.*

Here is another example of the power of the Holy Spirit. 2 Kings 13:20– 21 (KJV): *And Elisha died, and they buried him. And the bands of the Moabites invaded the* *land at the coming in of the year.* ***21*** *And it came to pass, as they were burying a man, that, behold, they spied a band of men; and they cast the man into the sepulcher of Elisha and when the man was let down and touched the bones of Elisha, he revived and stood up on his feet.*

Did we not say into the grave and beyond? That Spirit is the Spirit that the writers of the Book of Revelation discard and replace with mere mortals.

Comment: All the believers are sealed with the Spirit, from Abel all the way to the last person who will be called, before the kingdom comes and that is right on our doorsteps. Remember the **Matthew 24** Prophesy? *"When you see all these things come to pass, know that it is near even at the door."*

Now the reader may ask why we are spending all this time on the Holy Spirit. Here is the reason why. The writers of the Book of Revelation would have us believe that the Creator now communicates with the church with different system from the one he gave to the apostle John and all the other apostles. Being repetitious in getting this important concept across is after all the foundation from which to understand, that the Book of Revelation is a fraudulent work.

In the first chapter of the Book of Revelation, we are told this is the revelation of Jesus Christ which God gave to him, and He in turn gives this message to an Angel, and this Angel must now pass it on to John in a vision and then—even more absurd—tell John to write down everything he saw and then send it to the seven churches which are in Asia and do it by seven messengers. This way the Holy Spirit that seals us even beyond the grave has no more work to do since the ***seven*** human beings will now have this most important and urgent work to do from the Isle of Patmos.

They would obviously travel by boat over the Mediterranean Sea and hop on an ass (Donkey) or on foot, to continue their journey on the Asian Continent to the seven churches. How is that for utter nonsense? This should help you to grasp the magnitude of the fraudulent work of the writer(s) of the Book of Revelation.

John 14:15 (CJB): *If you love me, you will keep my commands;* **16** *and I will ask the Father and he will give you another comforting counselor like me; the Spirit of Truth to be with you forever.*

Again here we emphasize forever.

CHAPTER 5

RADICAL WRITERS

Just how radical were the writer or writers of the Book of Revelation?

Is colossal ignorance too strong to describe their actions, and by using those words, will it shock the reader to learn, just how far the writers of the book would stoop to present a book of false witness?

We will continue with our presentation by showing the reader how radical the writers of the Book of Revelation were when they concocted this nonsense which they call Revelation. The only thing they revealed is their ignorance of the scriptures.

In **John 3:13 (KJV):**

> *And no man hath ascended up to heaven, but he that came down from heaven, even the Son of man which is in heaven.*

That is a very clear statement with no mystery whatsoever. The Creator tells us that no man has ascended to heaven.

Note: Enoch and Elijah were long dead when the Messiah made that remark.

Who would doubt His word? If you happen to be an old Bible student, you may try to dispute that scripture based on your previous indoctrination regarding Enoch and Elijah, but you must realize they are not in heaven. Those words were spoken by the Messiah himself; surely he would know.

From Genesis we learn, all the years of Enoch were 365, and his life ended. In Chronicles, you will note that Elijah was on this Earth after he departed in a whirlwind.

In Revelation 5 and verse 3, the writer(s) records:

> *And no man in heaven, nor in earth, neither under the earth was able to open the book.*

From first Corinthians, the apostle reminded the congregation that if the dead rise not, eat, and drink, for tomorrow you die. Everything in your Bible hangs on the resurrection of the dead.

From Ecclesiastes 9:10, we learn

> *Whatsoever thy hand findeth to do, do it with thy might; for there is no work, nor device nor knowledge, nor wisdom in the grave wither thou goest.*

This begs a serious question: Who are the people in heaven? The writer tells us. Who could not open the book or look therein? Secondly how did they get there? The scriptures above tell us there is no knowledge or wisdom in the grave where the dead go.

Clearly then, the writers of the Book of Revelation contradicts the other passages in the Bible. Even the messiah was put in his grave when he died, where he awaited the resurrection from the dead.

In Revelation 6 and verse 9, the writer(s) tell us: *and when he had opened the sixth seal I saw under the altar the souls of them that were slain for the word of God.*

Ecclesiastes 9 and verse 5 reads as follows: *for the living, know that they shall die, but the dead know not anything. Again we find more lies written in the book.*

In the faith chapter, **Hebrews 11:13 from the CJB we read,** *All these people kept on* ***trusting*** *until they* ***died,*** *without receiving what had been promised* (first part) and now in the same chapter **verse 39,** *All of these had their merit attested because of their* ***trusting.*** *Nevertheless, they did not receive what had been promised.*

Note: There ***are no dead people in heaven, not then, not now.***

In chapter 20 and verse 12 in revelation, the writer states, "And I saw the dead small and great stand before God, and the books were opened," and the dead were judged out of the things written in the books. **The scriptures say the dead know not anything.**

Again we find more lies written in the book.

First Corinthian 15:23 (KJV): *But every man in his own order: Christ the first-fruits afterward they that are Christ's at his coming.* **Do you see the problem? The dead in Messiah are still dead; they come back to life when the Messiah returns.** More scriptures from Hebrews 9 and verse 27:

It is appointed unto all men once to die, but after this the judgment.

Clearly then, judgment comes at the time of the resurrection from the dead.

Finally verse 28:

> *So Messiah was once offered to bear the sins of many; and unto them that look for him, shall he appear the second time, without sin unto salvation.*

CHAPTER 6

MORE IMPOSSIBLE EVENTS...

We will now share with you more impossible events written in the book that are physically impossible. They should help you realize the scope of the madness of the people who were responsible for this book that bears the title Revelation.

It reveals the appalling ignorance of a people long dead, almost two millennia ago. One might even consider using the word *twisted* to describe them. Having made that very caustic statement, let us now look again at what the Bible says versus what is written in the Book of Revelation.

The Word *First-fruits* is not familiar to most of the English-speaking world of today, neither it is taught throughout the major religious organizations. Yet it is found written in thirty-two places in the Bible, including in the Book of Revelation in the Christian Bible. Why is this so, one might ask. And why do we not hear that word used in our churches? The simple answer is, Christianity teaches the Law of Moses is not for Christians. Well, that's true; however, in order to learn the origin of the word ***First-fruits*** and its usage in your Bible, it is necessary to learn about the **Law of Moses**.

In Exodus 23:14 (KJV), Moses wrote: *Three times thou shalt keep a feast unto me in the year **16** and the feast of harvest, the **First-fruits** of thy labors which thou hast sown in the field.* That is the first place in the Bible where we find that word written in connection with harvesting of the crops of the field under the law of Moses.

You are now asking at this point what has the Law of Moses got to do with the Book of Revelation. A great deal is your answer, and here is why. In **Acts 2:1,** we find the following words written: *and when the day of Pentecost (First-fruits) was fully come, they were all with one accord in one place.* Christianity wrongly records it Pentecost.

They were gathered together in one place to observe the **Feast of** *First- fruits*, **not Pentecost,** in observance of the Law of Moses. This was a biblical command to the children of Israel as evidenced in **Exodus 23:14** and elsewhere in Deuteronomy and Leviticus with reference to the Law of Moses. This was, after all, a Hebrew event, not a Christian event.

Very important note: There were no Christians in the Messiah's day. You cannot find the word "Christian" in any of the Gospels, and if you do, we highly recommend that you do some research and get a better translation of the Bible.

In Revelation 14:4 (KJV), we read**:**

*These are they which were not defiled with women; for they are virgins. These are they which follow the Lamb whithersoever he goes. These were redeemed from among men, being the **first-fruits** unto God and to the Lamb.*

The writer(s) of the Book of Revelation identify this group of 144,000 found in verse 1 as a group of men who were virgins in their previous life. They did not defile themselves with women. According to the writer/writers, even sex between married couples male/female defiles a man, not the woman, just the man, In the book of Hebrews 13:4, the Apostle Saul was inspired by the Creator to tell us that marriage is honorable and the bed <u>undefiled.</u>

In Genesis, Adam and Eve were told by the Creator to be fruitful and multiply, ***fill the earth!*** Here is another major blunder by the writer/writers of the Book of Revelation. The Creator commanded marriage to populate the earth. He inspired Saul to remind the Hebrew congregation that marriage is honorable and the bed undefiled. Yet the Revelation writer(s) tell us that marriage is dishonorable. It defiles men.

Time for a pointed question: Which religious organization practice celibacy among their leaders? We know, and so do you.

Let's continue to look at these celibate men who did not defile themselves, who disobeyed the command of the creator and did not marry. The writer tells us that these virgin males are the *First-fruits,* and they have been redeemed or harvested from among humanity. In the book of Acts on the day of Pentecost, in the church in Jerusalem the scriptures clearly show, men and women with no mention from the Apostle Pau/Saul that it was an all-male assembly. We know from the Gospels that there were women in the church.

In Acts 2:16 (KJV), Peter informed the people assembled on that day of the feast of first-fruits, *but this is that which was spoken by the Prophet Joel*, regarding the *last days* and the *pouring out of the Holy Spirit on all flesh* **verse 17**.

In **verse 39,** Peter had this to say to the people**.** *For the promise is unto you, and to your* ***Children****, and to all that are afar off, even as many as the LORD our God shall call.*

Note: We capitalized **Children** for emphasis. You are about to see why. In **verse 17,** he said,

And it shall come to pass in the last days, saith God, I will pour out of my Spirit upon ***all*** *flesh: and your* ***Sons*** *and your* ***Daughters*** *shall prophesy and your young men shall see visions and your old men shall dream dreams:*

Here in the book of Acts, we see that the church, the ***First-fruits***, consists of sons and daughters. The writer(s) of the Book of Revelation would have us believe when the Messiah returns and the dead are resurrected, the ***First- fruits*** if you will were actually a group of 144,000 virgin males (all the members of the church were virgin males?). Is that impossible? Yes, a resounding yes!

In 1 Corinthians 15:23, the Apostle Paul was inspired to write the following words: *But every man in his own order: Christ the* ***First-fruits;*** *afterward they that are Christ's at his coming.* **If that does not convince you** that the Book of **Revelation is a total fraud,** perhaps nothing can or will.

Now on to chapter 7 and the final insult from this book that we all have considered scripture for almost two millennia.

CHAPTER 7

A HISTORICAL APPROACH ...

The Book of Revelation was written in 96 AD/CE according to historical records. Since John was a contemporary of the Messiah, he would have been approaching his one hundredth birthday when he was given this assignment in 96 AD/CE.

In Revelation chapter 1 and verse **10,** the writer tells us that he received this vision while in the Spirit, on the **Lord's day.** A very fascinating revelation takes place when we search the Bible concordance to find another passage of scripture which supports the existence of the expression, **The Lord's Day.** That passage can only be found in the **Book of Revelation** according to Strong's exhaustive concordance.

The red flag gets raised at this time, and here is the reason why. In Christendom today, we know that the expression **The Lord's Day** is used in conjunction with the day of the week that bears the Roman calendar name, Sunday. Roman history also records that Roman Emperor Constantine on March 7 in the year 321 AD/CE declared Sunday as the official day of rest throughout the Roman Empire.

How could the Apostle John use that expression in writing the Book of Revelation in 96 AD/CE when the official day of rest was not made Roman law until the year 321 AD/CE? It was impossible for the Apostle John to be familiar with that expression. He was long dead by the year 321 AD/CE. It stands to reason, then, that it was impossible for him to be responsible for writing the Book of Revelation.

Here we have historical proof that the Book of Revelation is a total fraud. Not only did we show you from the scriptures that it was impossible for the Apostle John to have written the book. Now we have provided you with infallible historical proof. For centuries, church end-time doctrines have been fashioned or built around this fraudulent book.

Now that we have established that the Book of Revelation is a fraud, what do we do with the four horsemen of the Apocalypse, 666, the mark of the beast, the plagues, the destruction of one third of the Earth, etcetera, etcetera, etcetera? **We throw them out!**

If you have come this far, now you know what puzzled our predecessors for some 1700 years. You did not spend a lifetime or a day without success but less than two hours to learn the mystery of the Book of Revelation from the **Revelation of Revelation**.

Now, let's deal with what could be for some a daunting task. A radical forward step is needed if one chooses to accept the truth. If not, then all is nice and easy. Simply put, just go with the same old, same old. But for those who choose the former step as opposed to the latter, we are reminded that the Apostle Saul/Paul had this to say to Timothy in his second letter to him, *"All scripture is given by inspiration of God, and is profitable for* ***doctrine****, for* ***reproof****, for* ***correction****, for* ***instruction*** *in righteousness"* (II **Timothy 3:16 [KJV]**).

From the scriptures, we can make that radical step forward. We have the scriptures as our guide once again, as we pointed out at very start.

From Dr. David Stern's translation: The Complete Jewish Bible (CJB), Matt: 11:25.

It was at that time that Yeshua said, *I thank you Father, Lord of Heaven and earth, that you concealed these things, from the sophisticated and the educated, and revealed them to ordinary folks.* The KJV renders it the prudent and the wise.

Question: Are you one of those ordinary folks?

Scroll down to additional pages ...

THE REVELATION OF REVELATION MORE LIES

In Revelation chapter 21 and verse 1, the writer states: *And I saw a new heaven and a new earth.*

Note: *At this time* we caution the reader to be mindful of the fact that he, the writer, is seeing all this in a vision which he received from an angel which came from Jesus Christ which originated with the Father.

Here is the problem: In the year 698 BC, the word of the Lord (Jesus Christ) came to the Prophet Isaiah, and here is what we find written there.

Isaiah 65 and verse 17: *Look I create new heavens and a new earth.*

That passage was stolen from the book of the prophet Isaiah.

Do you see the problem? The writer here would have us believe that the Father/God has revealed to Jesus Christ who is also God, exactly what the Lord/Jesus (Christ/God) revealed to the prophet Isaiah more than seven hundred years prior to the writing of the Book of Revelation.

As we stated at the beginning of the book, God is God, and He does not reveal anything to God. John 10 and verse 30 reads, *I and my Father are one.* On to Corinthians where we can find scriptures that prove the Book of Revelation is a book of lies.

In Saul's letter to the Corinthian congregation, he stated the following:

From the CJB: Chapter 6 and verse 2: *Don't you know that God's People are going to judge the universe?* Verse 3: *Don't you know that we shall judge angels, not to mention affairs of everyday life?*

Saul/Paul made it abundantly clear that the church, made up of men and women, will be rulers of the world. **But**! In the Book of Revelation, the writer (s) tells us we will become Kings and Priests.

Notice: The women are removed just as they are removed from the 144,000 who are with the lamb on Mt. Zion. The ***all-male*** assembly made up of virgin males who did not defile themselves with women. The writer continues to tell us that they are first-fruits. See Revelation 14: 4.

Let's compare that passage with Rev 5 and verse 10. From the CJB, *You made them into a kingdom for God to rule Cohanim/Priests to serve him, and they will rule over the earth.* Note: The women are not there again. (Priests to serve him.) Here is a better rendering from the KJV. Rev 5:10: *And has made us unto our God kings and priests and we shall reign on the earth.* Again more lies; Saul tells us the church will judge the universe, ***males and females.***

Now to the book of Daniel for proof beyond any shadow of a doubt. Daniel 7 and verse 13 (KJV): *I saw in the night visions, and, behold, one like the Son of man came with the clouds of heaven, and came to the Ancient of days, and they brought him near before him.*

Verse 14: *And there was given him dominion, and glory, and a kingdom, that all people, nations, and languages, should serve him: his dominion is an everlasting dominion, which shall not pass away, and his kingdom shall not be destroyed.*

Verse 27: *And the kingdom and dominion, and the greatness of the kingdom under the whole heaven, shall be given to the people of the most High, whose kingdom is an everlasting kingdom, and all dominions shall serve and obey him.*

Note: Once again, we see there is no differentiation made. The scriptures clearly states to the people of the most High, not to a group of celibate males.

The Book of Revelation is a revelation of Lies as Brooke reminded us on the home page.

Comment: Throughout the Book of Revelation, we find the handwriting of a group of celibate males. Not only do we find the evidence of celibates, but also we find an emphasis of the church being addressed as brothers. Every letter that was written to any congregation we find the church being addressed as brothers when, in fact, the church was a body of believers from every gender. It is no small wonder that outsiders consider the church a male- dominated organization. The celibate presence clearly shows a group celibate males being responsible for most of the trash that we find throughout the New Testament. The King James translators were more respectful and used the word *Brethren*, indicating the family relationship of the males and females in the congregation.

www.ingramcontent.com/pod-product-compliance
Ingram Content Group UK Ltd.
Pitfield, Milton Keynes, MK11 3LW, UK
UKHW051133260726
13967UKWH00010B/3031

9 781954 341685